GARDEN POEMS

Other books by Douglas Atwill
from Boxwood Press

Bonfire
Douglas Atwill Houses
Fifty-Three Paintings
Seventy-One Poems
A Studio Year
Wings of Morning
Yellow Eyes in the Garden

GARDEN POEMS

Nature to Advantage Dressed

Also poems on Life, Death, Love, & Light-footedness

Douglas Atwill

BOXWOOD PRESS

Library of Congress Cataloging-in-Publication Data

Atwill, Douglas, author.
Garden Poems / by Douglas Atwill.

ISBN-13: 979-8670540834
Library of Congress Control Number: 2020914472

1. Poetry 2. Gardening 3. Gardens

Boxwood Press
PO Box 5959 Santa Fe NM 87502
505-983-2852
dougatwill@aol.com

Cover Painting:
Mixed Border on the Center Path. 29x23 Douglas Atwill
acrylic on Arches Bristol Board

Book design by Kathleen Dexter

CONTENTS

The new house was not quite finished when I moved in, much to the city building inspector's grief. Houses, in his mind, needed close inspection and approval before being occupied. But I was anxious to end the hiatus between houses and get going at the easel. In the end, I doubted that the city would enlist the aid of a sheriff or constable to take me struggling out of my own house, a construction permit scofflaw.

A few weeks later, the last inspection was finished with the production of the signed and vaunted CERTIFICATE OF OCCUPANCY. The unhappy inspector made me promise to never do this again. I promised and the contractor promised, as well.

By then a good portion of the new garden surrounding the house was in place. Walkways gave a sense of organization to the land, and stone-fronted terraces gave a Mediterranean finish to the large cut across the east boundary that we had to make to produce a flat place for the house. Fences, walls, and gates made for a sense of private enclosure, what the Romans called *hortus conclusus* – so necessary, in my mind, to a garden.

This was midsummer in 2019 and, with the able help of two strong men, we amended the soil, planted flowering shrubs, evergreens, perennials, apple trees, plums and peaches, shade trees, and plugs of thyme between the flagstones. As well as local providers, I found many nurseries online for such rarities as the yellow tree peonies and standard English roses. The irrigation system took several weeks to get installed, using water from the shared, very productive well.

By late September, everything was looking planted and happy, if sparse and separated far apart. I inspected it all regularly during the winter months, hoping that most of the new plants would survive.

It is now the following summer, and with only a few failures and bad choices, the garden is robust. (The Italian cypresses did not make it, nor did my Virginia tulip-tree saplings.) I have tried to capture the spirit of this project in these poems – the building of a new garden, the quiddities of it, and the qualms that woke me up in the night. Poems about other matters that occurred to me along the way have also been included.

There have been several dozen gardens for me before this one, so I was not without firm opinions as the project progressed. And now that this ncw one is starting into its childhood, I will watch it closely and see how well I have "nature to advantage dressed."

—Douglas Atwill
Santa Fe, July 2020

True Wit is Nature to advantage dress'd
What oft was thought, but ne'er so well express'd

—ALEXANDER POPE

Elysium

The old man decided
to build a new, more
thoughtfully designed, house
on a nearby lot, and
before it was even finished
he had started the new gardens
that would surround it,
his day-dreams full of stone-fronted
terraces overflowing
with trailing perennials, great
stands of fruit trees,
many of the favorite white peony
with a small crimson blaze,
a goodly number of the yellow
tree peonies nurseries were out of
the last time, the Asian boxwood that
stayed green all winter long and
everything else that had eluded him
in the many previous gardens,
plants perfectly spaced and
in the exact number of sunlit hours
that the lady garden-writers decree.
What could possibly
go wrong this time?

Laudate et Lilium

Lilies are agreeable plants,
being propagated by seed, scales, bulbils,
small pieces of the roots or stems, or
any part of the plant, and
they last for years, making bigger
clumps as they go along, and I have
read, I forget where,
anecdotes about their moving
themselves around
in a garden, hunting for more
suitable places to thrive,
creeping underground silently towards a
sunny patch or one with
better moisture, and I see
myself as distantly related to them, eons
ago sharing a perhaps pinnate-leaved grandfather, as
I move restlessly from house to house,
seeking my own better
patch in the sun.

Three-sided

Just outside the new studio
he planted the odd, brick-edged triangle, left over when
two garden borders adjoined at
an acute angle,
with what the package said was
one hundred thousand seeds of
Flanders Poppies, each as small
as a period on this page,
for what in his mind's eye
would be an early summer
mountain of red, surely enough
patterned groupings and cosmetic pairings for all
the garden paintings he could
expect,
even with his
cheery demeanor, to
paint in the years
that were left.

West-facing

The lot he purchased
for the new house was just
over an acre, with angled
sides like the keystone of an arch,
a gentle slope to the west,
reasonable southern exposure, and
the steep cut needed
to make a flat place for the house
he decided to terrace
with stair-stepped stone walls,
each of the four terraces
no more than three feet high, to
be planted thickly with lavenders,
flowering shrubs, roses,
columnar evergreens,
dwarf fruit trees and creepers
that would cascade down
across the stone walls and
before the house itself was
completed, the terraces were
already being planted lest
a moment be wasted of
the few years
he had left.

Walkways

For fifty years a painter
of gardens, among other subjects,
he had particular and strong opinions about
how a garden should be planted,
such as sharp angled paths between the borders,
of brick or stone or gravel,
to give a sense of regular geometry against
which to foil the abundant irregularity of
leaves, stems and blooms,
flat places for the eye to rest between
scanning the many-shaped leaves
and multi-colored blooms,
long pale-hued pathways to divide
and conquer the
flowery excess, a quiet
unmusical moment or two between the violins
and kettle-drums of symphonic
movements.

Cloven Hooves

It was early summer when
I moved into my new house,
the primordial garden borders and
stands of small fruit trees
seen with pride from every window and
glass door,
and I had mixed feelings
about the handsome herd
of six young bucks,
antlers aplenty,
who nibbled away on the
apple tree leaves and purple
plum foliage, looking
up without fear as I woke
with a snort in the lawn chair,
and I knew the added expense of
a tall fence was required,
no matter my keen appreciation
for their
excessive
creature beauty.

Thirty-six Months

Despite the wide acceptance that
generations-old gardens are
much-loved and respected,
the Hidcotes and the Villandrys,
he had observed that there is
something perfect in the third year
of a new garden, the clumps of iris thick with low clouds
of blooms, shrubs with enough be-flowered branches
to interweave, creepers that fall generously from
step to step, delphiniums that have not
used up the trace elements, before when
things need to be divided or cut back,
a new-born exuberance that no
older garden ever regains,
no matter how much tender care
and rearrangement in the
years that follow,
a sophomoric blush.

Fruit Tree

Good friends brought
by one evening
a housewarming gift of
a slim young tree,
a seven-foot apricot in
a two-gallon pot,
tags still attached,
looking like an
innocent, high-waisted
youngster with
long legs,
an orphan sent away
from danger
to the safe countryside,
awaiting the events
to come in his lifetime, from the
late April frosts, summer downpours,
lack of water in other years,
trunk-bending winds,
grasshopper swarms
and the incessant pecking beaks of
harvest-hungry birds in
the seldom-occurring
years of plenty,
his trunk circled with
the fallen fruit.

Notice on the Door

There is something
ominous and terrible
about the vicious red blooms
of the Oriental Poppies,
as they cut into the still air
of a late spring morning,
livid, luscious,
and I think that
they just might be
an early notice that
the Spanish Inquisition
has returned, with
their scarlet
emissaries just
around the corner,
collecting firewood
down the neighborhood
in long robes
and consulting
their maroon, Moroccan
leather register books,
unsmiling.

Wilted Shasta Daisies

There is a time each July,
sometimes as late as August,
when I look about
the garden where the peonies
have passed, the irises have
only their burnt-edged foliage to display
in a punishing sun,
all the peaches have been picked and eaten,
the Cox's Orange Pippins
have wormholes, the Bibb lettuces have gone
to seed in green towers, the gravel pathways
are overrun with sienna-colored ant hills and
invading layers of camomile,
the greengage plums are being stolen away by
blackbirds, and I wonder why
anyone of sound mind wants
a garden, wishing I had instead
paved the entire area in vintage red
herring-boned bricks with a reticulated
border like an Anatolian rug,
and I retreat
to the shaded house to
marinate myself in the
vinegar of despair, while I thumb through
the just-arrived nursery
color catalog with next year's featured
perennial, a wonderful creeping veronica
in a fetching shade of purple.

Dystopian Lunch

I have to admit
that kale has never been
a favorite of mine, but
because of the claims
of its indomitability,
something to eat when
the worst arrives, to keep
the neighbors and me going as
we get down to skin and bones,
I planted a few of them in the
vegetable rows, just to see,
and now
that winter has come,
their sturdy stems
are still upright in the snow,
unwilted,
undaunted,
unloved,
and very much
uneaten.

New Garden

Placing the new trees
and shrubs around the
areas of turned-over soil,
the gardener has a moment
of despair
at how lonely they look,
isolated,
without lines of boxwood,
drifts of perennials,
borders of iris and rock-edged pathways
to connect them,
to make them feel part of
a considered whole,
standing momentarily
alone in
the dry dirt.

Fairy Circle

There is a large,
at least century-old piñon tree in the
front of my new house,
crowded around with younger pines
and junipers, dark in its
impenetrable center with
saplings, a rotting tree-house
with ladder,
myriad groundcovers and
many-branched shrubs,
truly a thicket,
where I resist the
well-intended friends who call for
its sharp pruning, clearing
away the undergrowth, and
certainly undoing the tree-house,
lest I put an end to
the seasonal gatherings there
of the Other-folk who
bring good fortune
when I know
they must cluster
in its midst
on the nights
with a crescent
moon.

The Visitor

Somewhat early for his appointment,
Death, eschewing the doorbell
or the brass knocker,
chose to walk around and
wait it out in the back garden
until needed in the house,
making himself small enough
to hide under the boxwood,
keeping out of sight in the
shade, impatiently
turning healthy leaves brown,
dead-heading perfect blossoms
and
practicing his ancient skills
on the black beetles unfortunate
enough to scramble by,
until his expertise
was needed at
the main event
in the
master bedroom.

The English War

I imagine I
hear their voices
in unison in the terrace garden
on early summer mornings,
the pearl-necklaced, sun-hatted lady writers
of English garden books,
Vita, Rosemary, Penelope and Gertrude,
insisting with hissing scorn like
the many-tongued Oracle
of Delphi that I abandon
my foolhardy quest
to make an English
herbaceous border in this
low humidified, high summer-lighted,
alkaline-soiled, hailstone-prone,
spring-frosted, March-winded,
months-without-rain
country,
but some post-colonial rebel in me
made a low growl before
telling the ladies that the single perfect
blue delphinium standing up by
itself on the upper reaches
of my terrace garden,
seven thousand feet above the sea,
was surprisingly more beautiful than
a whole, descending border of them,

perfectly staked with straight sections of
green bamboo in the
soothing, salubrious, and easy mists of
East Grinstead.

Packed in Peat Moss

The tree nursery
was on Long Island and long-known
for superb espaliers –
seven-tiers,
candelabra, trellises,
and many others –
so I felt comfortable hearing
an older woman answer
in the business office,
with the gravelled voice
of experience and wisdom,
taking down my order for a
perfectly matched pair of Macintosh
three-tiers (our most popular selection, sir)
and a single
candelabrum of Arkansas Black
to be the focus at the end of a gravel walk
(all I could afford years ago in my
beginning, young garden),
personal check in the
mail today, please ship to my
house in
New Mexico, but this
duchess of horticulture
told me repeatedly
without interruption before
hanging up that they

never ship to
foreign countries.
Never.

32

Botanical Latin

The two
were on a first trip around
the north of England,
hunting down a famous old-rose nursery
in Shrewsbury,
walking around its ample display borders,
where ancient roses intermingled with shrubs
and new cultivars of perennial flowers,
when an old man nearby overheard
them talking, came over
to say, "You seem like
earnest young men,
with a keen interest in our gardens.
So may I suggest that you never utter
the words Beauty Bush again
as you just did, but
instead use the proper name
Kolkwitzia amabilis.
Otherwise, no one in
the higher circles of gardening
will pay you the smallest bit
of attention."
He made a decided military turn and
walked away, looking
back down at the small open
book in his hands.
So be it.

Forget Me Not

Fascinated by the ants I watch as I breakfast,
my observations lead me to make
broad statements about their particular doings.
One is that they have
no side-by-side friendships,
no buddies on their rounds,
and since most of them
are female, no girl-to-girl laughs and giggles
that you might hear in sororities or shirt factories.
If jokes come at all, they
come down tersely from on high, not like here
from the funny, fat woman stitching up a collar
at the next sewing machine.
Secondly, all decisions are made by consensus,
never by the ruler herself as in other kingdoms.
There is no Queen Anne deciding to decree
a nest-wide holiday on her birthday,
no free nectar today for all her subjects in the egg chambers,
no festoons with colorful leaf sections on the lower levels.
Thirdly, ants have no memory departments
in their brains, forgetting that well-marked pathway
to half-an-orange, dark with chomping ants,
after I wipe away with a soapy cloth the chemicals
marking their way there.
Instead, they have a few scouts forever wandering about,
racing back to the nest to breathlessly announce the new find,
a crumble of English muffin, a drop of marmalade,

or the self-same half-an-orange they
did not remember.
Overall, an odd life, I think, as I smugly smear
unsalted butter on the muffin.

Embowered in Pink

I had expected
a large crate from the
internet nursery,
potted roses,
all three of them the vigorous
climber named
"Eden,"
flower-filled summers
promised of pale pink,
roseate fragrance,
appearing again and again
along
its full twelve-foot height,
but only a small, light
package arrived in the post,
with three-inch by three-inch
pots of delicate stems
and shiny green leaves.
I realized I must
begin to look more closely
after my health
and make that extra effort to last for the
necessary decade
to see them crown the
garden gates.

Interrupted View

I've held for a
long time the notion
that houses are better
for the soul when encircled by
green borders, lines of flowering
shrubs, walls with climbing roses,
evergreens pruned for us to see over them,
herbaceous drifts,
small collections of trees,
with the
far view of mountains
beyond the garden wall,
pine-boughs like a fretwork
of green through
which to admire
the rising moon,
a garden like
a well-meaning friend blocking
the way between
us and the hard-edged
reality of the world
beyond.

Sack of Iris

They were there on the
front porch,
thirty rhizomes of
iris, delivered quietly
by an unknown friend
while I was napping,
a bulging grocery sack,
but now safely
planted in the full sun
on the
east terraces,
thinking their own
white-edged, deep-purple
thoughts
as I
give them a first
spray of water.

The Crowded Border

When the new garden
is almost planted,
the young plants all
a yard or two apart from each other,
the way experts say
is the only right way
to put in a new garden,
room to grow they say,
space for them to mature,
I cannot resist
putting more
plants between them,
to fill the space with green,
to see no naked soil
and earn the
title, once again, of
Mr. Overplant,
a wicked man
to the very bone.

Grass

The small rectangle
of grass,
rolls put down of Kentucky blue,
at first
seems out of place
in this dry climate, but
soon establishes its
own importance as
my own Piazza San Marco,
from which all
the pathways lead,
the very center of
the garden like
nothing else,
a verdant flat place,
better even than
a well-crafted
terrace of
herring-boned,
dusty-rose brick.

Bosworth Field

Because I
could not plant the bulbs myself,
time-worn knees in deep revolt,
the neighbor's son kindly
came to
help that day,
a stringy lad of good demeanor,
unschooled in matters of the earth,
and I used my cane to mark
the spots where he must plant,
unkindly not
trusting his youthful
ideas of
what makes a
fine spring border,
which I feared could be
long straight rows of
toy soldiers,
separate lines of yellows, reds and blues,
not the gentle mingle
of many colors I had in mind.

What Attractive Trumpet Flowers!

When a beginning gardener
first sees a spread of
bindweed, he might think
it a lucky arrival from his
neighbor's garden,
the strands of gray-green
heart-shaped leaves
sprouting small, white,
morning-glory-like flowers.
Let's leave it alone and see what
it does, but by then
it is too late, the
convolvulus arvensis spreading
rapaciously, more arms every day,
seeding with vigor
and sending the roots from its
rhizomes deep
into the soil where even
the sharpest fork cannot reach,
pushing out the more desirable
pansies and violets,
until it has surmounted
everything and owns
your land
and, even,
you.

Brass Hand

The widower down the street, a neighbor who always
seemed unhappy, scowling
even in the morning sun, planned to develop
the late Jennifer Anne's family house,
a gracious adobe set back from the street,
surrounded by mature perennial gardens, a house
he said needed to be torn down, to make room for the smaller
cottages more popular today.
We were surprised with his permission for us
to take what we wanted
before the heavy machinery arrived,
a hundred or so black bricks with mossy sides,
a few casement windows with bubbled glass, violet from their
many years in the sun,
an established row of a dozen white peonies with
a crimson blaze from the front garden
and the extra tall, ornate bedroom door, four beveled panels
with a brass knocker of a chubby woman's hand,
the Hand of Fatima in hardware parlance,
and I wondered who it was
who needed to knock before coming
into the bedroom – the morning
maid with breakfast on a tray or the
husband himself, on nights
of the black dog, when
nothing suited him and all was blackness.
Just how, I hesitated to ask him,
did Jennifer Anne die?

Fastigate

Since I often passed
and admired what I supposed was
a single, tall Italian cypress on
a nearby street,
even though the experts insist
we live far too north for
them to thrive,
or even to survive,
I ordered five
from a California nursery,
and planted them in a comely grouping
on the east terrace,
green fingers pointing to the stars,
a place for Tuscan red wine
and ribald stories.
Alas, none of them
wintered over to
prove me right.

Spider

To the small, black spider
scurrying across the travertine
floor of the expansive bathroom,
from the shower door all the way
across to the vanity,
it is a place as large
and dangerous as
the large Square in Beijing,
with the impending
descent of a giant bedroom
slipper in the sky overhead, or
a falling bar of lavender soap
the size of a zeppelin,
and innumerable
other household hazards
until he at last reaches
the partial safety of
cabinet, pulling himself up
as flat as he can against
the wall, somewhat
away from so many
sources of harm,
breathless,
watchful,
and
happy to have
made it.

Symmetry

Especially as I
get older and unlikely
to kneel down for
a gardening task,
I have learned to
appreciate tree roses,
where the blossoms are higher
up, waist-high,
easier to see,
more simple to prune
and take care of.
Also, there are the fond echoes
of times gone by when
tree roses
were planted regularly
in symmetrical
pairs on either side
of gray stone walkways,
three people wide,
for the delectation of
afternoon strollers
with top-hats and black umbrellas.

Grown from Seed

I try to think where
a plant that I liked in the garden
of a house I sold long ago
might be now,
a peony grown from seed
which took three years to
come into blossom, and was,
by the sheerest chance, a
white, double beauty with a single
pink petal, which I
named Mary Louise,
as is the right of the
hybridizer,
even the accidental one,
and had the good
fortune to deliver the
first bloom to her
at the evening cocktail hour,
when the fragrance was just coming
into its own.

Yellow Changes

It is early October and
the view from my studio windows
is turning gold.
This year the aspens
are a ruddy shade of ochre,
while the privets
have picked out the palest of yellows,
just one step away from pure white,
a tired, thin aureate wash over silver.
With the events of summer behind them,
all are more world-weary
than the
innocent spring yellows
of jonquils and buttercups, when
anything is possible in
the year to come.

Wishful Thinking

If you have had the luck
to have had a great love,
to have had the sleepless nights,
and to have the great misfortune
to watch him die
on a gray November morning,
you wonder in the years that
follow, why he could
not have
gone on, survived
until another springtime, like
the two dozen King Alfred daffodils
you planted together,
seen in many hundreds
through the fence
each year
down the street
in the green backyard
now owned by another.

Seeds in the Mail

He planted a closely-spaced row of the
Formosan Lily seeds in the cold-frame,
and by spring there were hundreds
of small grass-like plants,
which he carefully replanted farther
apart in a garden bed,
called pricking out
by the greenhouse people,
and by late that summer
there were several
ghostly white,
uncertain blooms,
but by September of the
following year, they all had grown
supple, strong stems
five and six feet tall,
topped with crowds of white trumpets so
fragrant that he was kept awake
well past midnight in
the third-story bedroom,
smiling in the dark.

In the Foggy Highlands

There is an anecdote
about a plant-loving
man named Bartram who in all weather
explored the Appalachians
in the late 1700s, searching for something new,
and in the mists he came upon
a magnolia tree
growing in the filtered light
of larger trees, high in the hills,
with shiny, green leaves longer
than his arm and seed pods
as big as teapots, which he
collected in his rucksack,
but lost when he slipped and
fell down at a fording place,
the scarlet seeds floating away
downstream.
He named his find
Magnolia Grandifolia,
the very mention of which brought
ridicule at horticultural society
dinners back in Philadelphia,
big leaves indeed,
laughter going on until well after the coffee.
Alas, nobody else
found it again, including
the man himself
on several return trips.

Alhambra Memories

He kept ordering
various varieties of
Magnolia trees from the
east-coast nurseries, hoping
to prove wrong the dire
warnings of garden books,
that none of them would take to the
western mountain soil and worrisome weather.
He pined for the
long crescent of magnolias planted
close together
at his grandfather's California house
(before it was torn down)
and the eleven-year-old's delight
when his cousin chased him
in fast curves between them,
breathless, laughing and
brushing against the dark,
glossy leaves with
bristly, sienna undersides.

Chinese Sister

I was interested to learn
that many typical North American,
New World plants,
like dogwood,
hollies, rhododendrons, cherry trees,
magnolias, maples, spruces, deciduous azaleas,
tulip-trees, persimmons,
and bog orchids
have another, similar
version native to China,
pulled away for eons from their siblings
by the last Ice Age, making small
changes during the long wait.
In my home country
I now
inspect their blossoms or branches for
hidden signs of Asia,
an odd, woody fragrance,
a particular upward curl of leaf,
or a way of making
strange, tinkling sounds
in the wind.

No Chirping

As dark approaches,
I sit outside the kitchen doors
and watch the birds arriving,
first taking a drink in the
bowl filled with water,
then finding an interior branch in the
crowded piñon circle,
to hide from the
circling owls,
or other top-of-the-list
raptors,
quiet as death in the night,
next to their
brothers and sisters
and cousins,
safe until the
changing light of
dawn,
when I suspect they
fly over to take another drink
and are then off for
the business of the day.

Double Siesta

A pair of does has discovered the
thicket just south of the
kitchen garden as a
place to sleep in the
afternoon,
hunkered down in the cool shade,
pine needles in a soft layer,
perhaps sisters making a
life together,
waiting until the
first breeze of evening to
smooth the cant of
their sibling's ears,
rustle the sleep-marked skin
and rejoin the world,
when the others also emerge
from their hiding
for the gloaming
frolic and to pass around the tales of
what happened during
the heat of day,
in the quiet language only
they can hear.

To Forgive

The *ailanthus*
is a most magnanimous tree,
dropping all the
collected clusters of summer slights
on the first frosty night
in October,
every leaf down on the
ground in a
muffled, merciful, midnight rain,
all the summer
misdeeds of others forgiven,
for the wintry weeks of peace
until the spring when
the green grudges
grow anew.

Malus Oceanus

On occasions I have
almost the same dream about a summer
I spent on the Penobscot Peninsula
years ago, painting outside
every day, selling the canvases each night
to the others at the white clapboard inn,
twenty dollars apiece,
exploring the
hidden coves, swatting insects,
sometimes swimming in the cold sea, and
in the dream I recall something
my mind tells my awake self
could not have been so,
a cluster of old, gnarled apple trees,
branches no higher than me,
growing right above the salt water,
green apples aplenty,
with large, tubular roots first coursing among
the rocks and then right down into the
clear sea, disappearing in the
deeper water. The dream may be
calling to me to take my
folding easel back there,
sell the small paintings
each night, and
see if I can find my brave-hearted
apple trees again.

Garden Passage

The six tree peonies
arrived in a box cushioned
in sphagnum moss,
and
we planted them with buds facing upwards,
three together at the end of one
border and three at the end
of the next border,
a flagstone walk between them,
like thriving seaports on two
nearby tropical islands,
close enough together to wave at
the selfsame others on the far shores,
and to see the double, yellow blossoms
from a single
boat passing slowly through
the narrows, looking
first left then right.

A Row of New Windows

My friend, sometimes
beloved and other times
a pain in the neck,
had the rare ability to
see when men are too, too masculine,
chewing tobacco and using
bad language,
they often
are just the opposite,
hiding a girlish reality beneath,
so when the quartet of men
in stained overalls
arrived at his studio with their concrete saws,
scuffing their steel-toed shoes as they walked,
scratching their crotches,
stomping out cigar butts,
ready to cut
noisily the new openings in
his solid block wall,
he said,
"Listen up, girls,
let's get something
straightened out
from the start."
The four of them
squealed with
delight at being

found out and became
fast friends to share
a glass of white wine.

84

Quavering Mind

As the time in autumn for planting
anything new in the garden
had all but passed,
the Mr. Equality in my brain
started to worry that I had
not made equal choices
for the colors of iris across
the garden, that there
were many more blues, violets
and purples, and that I had under-ordered
the yellows, oranges and pinks,
to say nothing of the ivories, plicatas and whites,
but then the Mr. Sensible who was also
lurking in my mind said that
a garden was no place
for this sort of democracy,
that the tyrant gardener could
choose as he wished in his own kingdom,
cosseting favorites and
giving away wealth to the most handsome,
banishing others forever, willy nilly,
so just before
the first freeze of fall, I uneasily put
in another order for a dozen Caesar's Brother,
the deepest purple of purple Siberian iris, to
sit beside me, without shame,
on the throne.

Needlessly Unhappy

Why is it that
in my garden I want to push the envelope,
to put a Zone Six
plant in my Zone Five garden,
to see if the Mediterranean fig, so happy
much farther south would
thrive here, if I plant it
against a south-facing wall
or in a corner out of the wind,
somewhat safe from winter storms,
instead of being
satisfied with the hardy Canadian Plums
or winter worthy apples and pears
in the gardens of neighbors?
It could be yet another
instance of a lifelong fight with
authority, always rankling when
told to what to do, or is it
a simpler wish to partake in a small
way of the glories of the
the warmer southern climes,
where a single breadfruit tree
can feed a village and fallen mangos
cover the ground, bees buzzing?

Cumberland County

It was the far end
of the county, where adjoining
farm families had sold up to the
timber companies and moved away,
and in the spring,
it was a pleasant hike for us through
the woods to the abandoned
sites of the farmhouses,
where the gentle climate of the
Virginia hills had kept alive
old lilac bushes, rows of
pale irises, small daffodils in downhill drifts,
and deep red, thin-leaved peonies in the
green-grassed clearings where
the houses once stood, sometimes
with a single, freestanding, brick chimney
or flower beds edged with river-rocks
and we summoned in our minds
what the families who planted
them must have thought as
they drove away in their autos for the last
time, some in tears, with tables and chairs
lashed to the roof,
but others, laughing, with the canvas top down,
a wicker hamper with fried chicken
and ham biscuits ready for the picnic later in the day
in a shady spot on their way
to a fine new life in the north.

Country Days

It was the Sixties,
when the youth of America
was clamoring for change, but
we were hidden away deep
in the rolling hills,
in a stately red brick house with
no television, no radio,
unaware of the revolution,
reading aloud to one
another from modern English
novels and
gardening books as the
oak fires crackled,
baking apple pies and
corn-meal muffins,
roasting butter-covered chickens,
assured that
our love would
last a lifetime,
just like the old
house, and
that the marching lines
of change might
just wear themselves
out before they came down
our road and we
were discovered.

Promises, Promises

There is a time
in late winter or
very early spring when
the border is coming
alive again, tufts of
leaves in all
manner of green,
too soon for flowers,
but exuding a
splendid promise of
the floraison to come,
images of double peonies that
do not fall in the rain,
roses without a single beetle,
delphiniums that do not
bend in the breeze, and
the overarching surety
that everything good
is possible.

If It Please, Your Honor

Somewhere in the Old World,
in the massive central highlands of France or a
cathedral town in England,
there is rumored to be a particular
courtroom where horticultural
misdeeds are prosecuted,
a paneled room the color of lettuce where
the judges wear robes
piped in forest-green gimp,
tulip-shaped hats on their heads, and
law-books of viridian leather open before them,
passing severe, time-honored judgments
upon garden scofflaws such as I,
waiting in stern silence
until the world grants
them the power to extradite me
from a New World nation where anything goes
in the garden,
any color next to another,
sword-shaped leaves among the filigreed,
and tall plants happy
at the front of the border,
blocking view of the short
ones farther back.
Ordered to appear and
guilty as charged.

Iberis Calor

The skunk cabbage,
besides being a nauseous
harbinger of spring,
has the remarkable ability
to melt the surrounding snow,
and thus push up an early, frigid blossom,
so why cannot we
cross this cabbage with a more
amenable plant like the
candytuft, so often planted
beside entry walks,
bestowing the gift of
an ice-free pathway in January
as well as
white blossoms in the
summer months?

Golden Wishes

While thinking about snow,
there is a tale brought back by
those who spend time at the monasteries
in the Himalayan approaches,
of the lamas who sit cross-legged and
silent throughout the year on
the high hills,
and with their minds alone
melt the winter snow
away in a wide circle around them
(without so much as a whiskbroom),
and I wish I could buy
a discount plane ticket
for one of them to come
west and talk,
lama-to-plant,
to the Lady Bank's Rose, giving up
to her his survival secrets, so
in my northern garden
I could plant her divine
and abundant
yellowness on my garden gate,
and think thankfully of Buddha.

Liriodendron

Four tulip trees arrived
in a small parcel,
each a single trunk
no bigger than a pencil,
and it takes a great
stretch to see them
as the grown trees
I remembered
on the verges of
Virginia forests,
straight trunks
up and up, first
branch twenty feet
high, but
covered with
the early summer
orange and yellow blossoms,
and, if happy,
growing in a century to
two hundred feet
for my child's child's
child.

Night Visitor

Last night I dreamt
that he came for me in the night,
saying that it was time to come, my love,
we have been apart for far too long,
that there was another place for me,
but I told him
right off
I had those undone
things here
that I needed
to do beforehand,
but please refrain
from giving away my spot
to anyone else,
and, now in the harsh light of day,
I question my hasty, maybe foolish,
choice for the terrestrial everyday over
the ethereal, loving unknown.

Druid's Place

It was a long
walk away from the house
on the narrow path
through woods filled with
underbrush, prickly shrubs, thick
with saplings and seedlings
of all manner, to
the clear circle in
the grove of smooth beech trees,
the valiant princes of them all,
a clearing with only
the soft mat of last year's leaves,
no weeds or green intrusions,
echoes of the ancient meetings held there,
eyes seeming to follow us from the
dark verges beyond the circle,
the light gray trunks
like elephant's legs,
a place to lie down
among them
and feel at one.

Red Triangle

We double-dug the soil
in the three-sided, brick-edged bed,
mixed in the soil amendments
between the lawn and the copse of young trees,
and sowed the tens of thousands of tiny seeds,
each smaller than the mark of a sharp pencil,
raking the surface with the special Japanese rake,
in hopes of making the
summer explosion of red corn poppies,
that are
sometimes grumpy
about germinating in a private garden
(but always annoyingly happy in an open Flanders field),
and wait, watering when needed,
fingers-crossed for the first signs,
for the warm day's return,
promising scarlet success.

AEGEAN STORM II   ATWILL

Aegean Dreams

Sleep well tonight,
my dear,
with three pillows
under your fair head,
a smoothness of linen against the night's chill,
a deep sleep without
waking moments,
and tomorrow we
will rise and
wash together,
eat slices of brown bread
and sections of blood orange,
then walk with care down
the rocky path to the sea,
and swim away
across the shallow
lagoon to
the next island,
even now beckoning
to us on the horizon.

Permission Denied

I once had
a long row of delphinium
in an otherwise
vegetable-filled garden,
a line of blue-eyed beauties
who lofted over the
lettuce and the chives,
making me proud
beyond my due,
making me think of the
Macedonian king whose nine daughters
brought suitors from other
kingdoms across
the sea, with promises of
wealth and happiness in their
far lands, if the king
would just give his blessing,
and I understood
why he refused all their offers,
to grow old in comfort with
the nine, comely offspring
at his side.

To Share

Because my
newly planted garden
is without a
circumferential fence,
I expect that
next spring I must
divvy up the first tender leaves on
the apple trees and the
succulent early stems of tulips as they rise
out of the ground
for the small herd
of deer that wander
about my end of town,
until I give up being
benign and generous,
and complete
the circle of latillas.

Purple Blossoms

On the first
day of February,
I search around for the upward,
green points of bulbs
planted while on aging knees
in the last
days of September,
hoping they have survived
the many dangers of being
all winter underground,
the munching teeth, the
odd fungus, or the
overweaning, crippling
moisture
to grow higher
and fulfill the basic
and underlying garden promise
that the good is stronger
than the rot.

No Beets This Year

There is no vegetable
garden in my current house,
unlike the central plot of rows
in my last house, edged smartly in sienna-colored stone,
crowded with
lettuces of many colors, onions,
garlic, carrots, sometime a beet or two,
potatoes, peppers and kale,
and always a stand of corn,
making its rustling noises at night,
and in odd moments, I feel a sense of
guilt about the lack,
that eons of forebears are
finding fault with my
flowery and irresponsible terraces, just
now coming into full bloom,
a frivolous bagatelle that
the town fathers would
have forbidden
had they known.

Mea Culpa

In thinking about the
absence of things to eat from
my garden,
I wonder if I might
plant some heads of cabbage
amid the lavender,
carrots among the roses,
tomatoes against the south-facing wall,
clusters of onions to give
height to the creeping campanula,
and a long crescent of corn on
the topmost terrace,
to impart an air of culinary substance
to my otherwise
good-for-nothing garden,
bringing half-hearted smiles
of approval
from the town fathers.

Family Outing

At breakfast on the day of their departure
his fearless mother-in-law
said he was much too inexperienced and honest
to smuggle the nuts through the Orly Airport,
or to lie convincingly to the sharp-eyed
agricultural agents across the sea,
so she would take the forbidden horsechestnuts
they had all—the lover, his mother, himself—
picked up while strolling under the trees
in chateau gardens on a fall family trip abroad.
The nuts survived in a dark,
damp part of her large purse,
the imposing woman unquestioned,
allowing him to plant them,
already with first roots pushing out,
in the glassed potting shed,
a foot high by the end of the next year,
to nurture them through the early years,
and now the dozen of them mostly forty feet high
and forty-five years old with impressive trunks,
all in different gardens across
the eastside of town, and
in the spring when they are in candle,
lover and mother gone,
he drives by them, one after
the other, pausing, motor idling,
and remembers mother and son
had the same fierce blue eyes.

Fall from Grace

In my dream
I had almost fluent
French,
walking with aplomb around
the sitting room of the Countess D'Vray,
who claimed I spoke with an odd Moroccan overtone
with an even more odd preference for the subjunctive,
which charmed all her guests,
belying my West Texas origins and nurturing
rumors of connections to royal houses
of the coast,
that my hostess wickedly encouraged with tales of
her secret search revealing
a jeweled scimitar amid the luggage
in my guest quarters,
as well as a baroque pearl clip for a turban,
so when I awoke in
quite another type of world,
all that remained of my
Francolingual glory
was to greet my beloved
with
"Bonjour, mon pussycat."

Late Afternoon

The afternoon light through
the trees made green polygons
on the kitchen wall, a
cool breeze coursing
through the house,
as he waited for her to arrive,
customarily late for their
get-togethers,
a yoga class running too late,
or bit of computer work taking longer
than she thought,
and she brought the bottle
of cold Chablis, which they
shared on the back garden loggia,
wedging a small piece of wood under
the wobbly table leg,
laughing at her week's adventures
and his stories of long ago,
while the garden watched them and
a small rabbit munched
on the coreopsis blossoms and
sharp points of the
delphinium leaves.

ACKNOWLEDGEMENTS

It would be a difficult task to put together this collection without the friends and associates who are so helpful along the way. Brad Richardson and Doug Gruenau listened as I read these poems aloud, on many occasions. Walter Cooper and Doug Bland also read and corrected snippets as I wrote them. I talked about the gardens with Billy Halsted and Wayne Bladh, comparing our parallel endeavors. Wendy Schiller read the poems with a sharp pencil in her hand, questioning when I went too far afield. Kathleen Dexter completed the book design with her usual expertise, omitting an ill-used word here and there. And I have to give thanks to my long departed partner, Victor (Pete) Stewart, for getting me started in the world of gardens. In the late 1960s we traipsed up and down the U.S. East Coast, UK, and south of France in search of ideas for our Virginia garden, and found many.